Tributes

to

Swami Dayanand Saraswati

(The Indian Renaissance Rishi)

Edited with English Translation
By
Dr. Ravi Prakash Arya

Amazon Books, USA

In associationwith

Indian Foundation for Vedic Science
1051, Sector-1, Rohtak, Haryana, India
Ph. 09313033917; 09650183260
Email : vedicscience@rediffmail.com
vedicscience@hotmail.com
Web : www.vedicscience.net

Second Edition

Kali era 5116 (c. 2014)
Kalpa era 1,97,29,49,116
Brahma era 15,55,21,97,29,49,116

ISBN 81- 87710-74-8

© **Authors**

All rights are reserved. No part of this work may be reproduced or copied in any form or by any means without written permission from the authors.

Contents

	Pages
Editorial	4
Tributes paid by Hindi Papers	27
Tributes paid by Urdu Papers	48
Tributes paid by English Papers	67
Tributes paid by Bangla Papers	95
Tributes paid by Bilingual Papers	96
Tributes paid by Gujrati Papers	99
Tributes paid by Marathi Papers	111
References	116
Rare Pictures of Rishi Dayanand	117

Editorial

Today the burning issues before the modern world are growing poverty (hunger), exploitation of poor and deprived, environmental pollution, communalism, religious bigotry, terrorism, discrimination of human beings on the basis of gender, colour, creed, race, region or religion. Rishi Dayanand was a great seer of the modem age. He was the *Yuga draṣṭā* (Renaissance Rishi) and *Viśva Guru* (World teacher). He could visualise all these problems of the modern world in the middle of the 19th century itself and gave an amicable solution to all such problems that the world was likely to face in the years to come. The solution was given by him in the form of ten principles of Arya Samaj, *Satyartha Prakash* and many other books written in conformity with Vedas. He discarded the various religious sects in the name of *Mata* and *Matantaras* and set into motion a new movement in the name of Arya Samaj (academic, social, and spiritual agenda of reforms) in 1875 with the Vedic motive of '*kṛṇvanto viśvam āryam*', to make the whole world noble and civilised, to purge the modern world of its various ailments and notions for the coexistence of human beings on the globe, to remove poverty, exploitation, communalism, religious bigotry, discrimination of human beings and to create social and environmental awareness. Initially, he was not willing to give any name to his movement for the fear of its being branded as a religion (religious sect) like others in the world.

In addition to above, Rishi Dayanand was a reveller of the truth. His magnum opus *Sathyartha Prakash* "Revealing the Truth" is a glaring example of this fact. His contribution may also be counted towards shaping the prosperous, enmity free modern world of friendship and fraternity. First time in the modern history of humankind he put forward the principles of coexistence. He was a staunch advocate of Vedic Altruistic Socialism, Altruistic Nationalism or Internationalism.

Rishi Dayanand's life was an ideal example of a good citizen. The concept of good man has been distinguished from the concept of a good citizen. A good man is endowed with good personal qualities, but he has no role to play in the society and national development except that he is a good man. In other words, a good man is a passive person who neither acts nor reacts to what is happening in the society. But a good citizen is an active person who reacts with good or bad happening in the society. A good citizen has the guts to declare wrong as wrong and right as right without any regard to his selfish interests. Rishi Dayanand was a good citizen. He never hesitated to point out rights and wrongs of British rulers and the Indian society irrespective of gender, caste, creed, region and religion. He was a person who praised the Queen for her justice but when the British Viceroy asked him to praise the British rule in his public lectures, he plainly refused to do so and spoke candidly to British Viceroy that it is better to live in a self-ruled State howsoever bad it is than to live under a good State ruled by foreigners. Once when his attention was drawn to the unhappiness of British rulers for his comments, Dayanand says: I have no fear from any ruler or king so far as the exposition and propagation of truth are concerned. Thus Rishi Dayanand's life teaches one to be a good citizen of one's own country. This notion lies in line with the Rgveda's slogan *vayam rāṣṭre jāgriyām purohitāḥ* 'Let us be awakened like a leader/ good citizen in the nation.

Rishi Dayanand was a staunch exponent of Altruistic Welfare in the Call for Globalisation. Today the entire World is talking about globalisation under the pressure of America. The American concept of globalisation is based upon the exploitation of weak and poor nations for selfish interest or say for further enriching its capital. This type of capitalist globalisation will prove fatal for humanity at large especially for poor and developing nations. Long back in the middle of 19th century, Dayanand also advocated globalisation, but his concept of globalisation was based upon two principles (1). The well-being of the entire world as advocated by him in the 6th principle of Arya Samaj (The welfare of the entire world should be our aim). He defines the term welfare or *upakāra* as the promotion of physical, spiritual and social well-being).

According to Swami Dayanand, an Individual person's welfare lies in the welfare of entire society. Similarly, a nation's welfare lies in the welfare all nations. He advocates in the 9th principle of Arya Samaj (An Individual's welfare lies in the welfare of whole Society). These principles, if followed in a campaign of globalisation, will change the entire look of the world.

With the rise of socialism in the world the concept of a welfare state came to a forefront in a democratic set up to curtail the capitalism. The American concept of a welfare state curtails capitalism within its internal setup since it is not based upon the exploitation of its own citizens. It gives rise to another type of capitalism which is based upon the exploitation of poor, developing and under developed nations. Dayanand's welfare State in the light of the 6th and 9th principle of Arya Samaj becomes the real welfare state which not only considers the welfare of its own citizen but the welfare of the other poor nations in the world. The Veda says: *kevalāgho bhavati kevalādi,* i.e, a person/nation who eats alone eats sin. The Vedic prayer in Hindi also reads as follows: *bhukhā pyāsā paḍā paḍausi tune roṭi khāi to kyā.* 'There is no greatness in filling up one's own stomach if the neighbour is suffering from hunger and thrust. 'Today's capitalist countries would like to throw their surplus grain to oceans instead of transferring them to the needy and poor countries. The real welfare state in a democratic set up can be created only by following the principles of Rishi Dayanand.

Today's India can benefit a lot from Rishi Dayanand's vision for developed and prosperous India. He was the first practitioner of applied democracy in India. He was the first to introduce the element of election in Arya Samaj in 1875. Keeping in view the instability of Government in a democratic set in India, we may follow the great visionary saint Rishi Dayanand. He on the basis of the statement of the Vedas stressed the element of election. King, as he interprets, is to be the president of the assembly. According to him, the wisest and the most learned among the members of an assembly is to be elected the king or the president. Thus he provides a tangible solution to the present crisis of instability of the Government of India in the parliamentary form of Government. According to him, the prime minister should be elected by the parliament and not by the party. If this norm is made prevalent there will be no instability of the Government for five years. In parliament, the prime minister may be voted out and not the Government. Another prime minister will be elected irrespective of consideration of majority or minority and the stability of the Government will he ensured and there will be no need for re-elections or midterm polls.

Dayanand's nationalism discards the radical nationalism prevalent today and supports altruistic nationalism which is based upon the internationalism. He is a nationalist in the world perspective. His concept of nationalism does not stand at the cost of other nations. He introduces the idea of life and helps others to live. He does not like to overlook his national interest but at the same time, he does not want to interfere with others' interest. According to the 10th principle of Arya Samaj: An individual should be free to act so far as individual welfare is concerned but should not act freely so far as altruistic welfare (welfare of all individuals/ persons/ or nations) is concerned. He is not in favour of the kind of nationalism prevalent in America where one's own national interests are carried out at the costs of other nations. For our own progress, we cannot exploit others.

Founder of Dharma: Krishna in Gita tells Arjuna: *dharma sansthāpanārthāya sambhavāmi yuge yuge.* "The People like me take birth to finding the lost *Dharma, yuga* after *yuga.* Thus after Krishna, it was Rishi Dayanand who founded the lost *Dharma.* Today *Dharma* has been replaced by religion. According to Dayanand, *Dharma* is not a religion but eternal laws and human values based upon the truth which sustains universe and biological and human life on the earth. He himself defines *Dharma* in the fifth principle of Arya Samaj as 'We all should act according to *Dharma.* i.e. with the consideration of what is truth and what is an untruth.' Thus his *Dharma* or Vedic concept of *Dharma* propagated by him was not the concept of a religion created by human beings just like different religions of the present day. Dayanand never trusted man-made things since human beings create things for their selfish purposes. Man made rules, or things cannot address the universal problems. Since they have a limited range and limited things do not have universality in them. Dayanand's *Dharma* is the fountainhead of Science. He never accepted the things in the name of religion. According to him, Vedas were not the religious books like Bible or Koran rather they are the books of all true sciences and knowledge. He quotes Yaska : *sakṣāt kṛt dharmāṇo ṛṣayo babhuvu*, i.e. 'There were born Rishis to whom was revealed the entire knowledge'. Thus his *Dharma* is not immune of science, whereas the religion, as we have seen presently and in the past, has been the antithesis of science. To top it all, he could visualise that all these religions are the business shops marketing human beings. The religions are dividing human beings from human beings by way of their vicious agendas, rituals, dress codes, a way of worship and propaganda. That is why he discarded the idea of the existence of religious sects or *Matas*. In the 12th, 13th and 14th chapter of *Satyārtha Prakāśa* he made an attempt to reform the religions to make them more pro-science or knowledge based. He raped all these bigoted religions prevalent in the world whose business is thriving upon innocent human beings. These religions are the root cause of various altercations and terrorism in the world. Today we have been talking about interfaith dialogues. But following Rishi Dayanand's notion, I would emphasise that today the need is not for the interfaith dialogues but the faithless dialogues. If we want the true welfare of the humankind on the earth, we shall have to discard all these religions out-rightly. If the world wants to survive the destruction caused by quarrels of religions and terrorism propelled by religions, religions would have to be discouraged (as done by Rishi Dayanand) and replaced by spirituality and the Vedic concept of *Dharma* would have to be followed in true spirit.

Here it may not be odd to inform that Vedic concept of *Dharma* is based upon Spirituality. Spirituality informs us that entire humanity is one. What to say of humanity, all creatures are the creation of God. As such killing even of an animal is a crime. That is why Rishi Dayanand propagated vegetarianism. He was so confirmed about it that he even avoided sharing meals at the houses of non-vegetarians.

Dayanand's Vedic Altruistic Socialism: Dayanand's Vedic Altruistic socialism is similar to Marxian scientific socialism so far as Marx advocates that the right given to an individual in the socialistic set up are not for the benefit of the individual alone but for the benefit of the entire society. According to Rishi Dayanand (9th Principle of Arya Samaj), an individual /person or nation should not content with his/her own welfare but an individual person's/nation's welfare lies in the welfare of all individuals/nations. Marx's Scientific Socialism is based on the principles of cause and effect. He discards religion whereas Rishi Dayanand brings *Dharma* in its true form of spirituality and human values in his socialism.

Staunch Exponent of Scientific Awareness: Today we have ushered in the era of science. For the true advancement of science, scientific awareness is mandatory. Howsoever, the scientific advancement takes place in the world, but so far as the scientific awareness is lacking, a society cannot be said to be scientifically advanced in the real sense of terms. Rishi Dayanand lays the foundation of scientific awareness among human beings, by coining the fourth principle of Arya Samaj. He observes: 'One should always be ready to accept the truth and give up untruth'. The concept of truth is the underlying factor for scientific awareness. First time in the human history we find such a principle that advocates adherence to truth without following any religious dogma. There are so many examples in the history where truth was suppressed in the name of religion. According to the fifth principle of Arya Samaj, 'All should perform their actions according to *Dharma* i.e. with the consideration of truth or untruth. Long back in human history, Rishi Dayanand came on the stage and asked people to accept what is scientific (true) and discard what is unscientific, as the human society in those times was dominated by all dogmatic religions and people were forced to accept what was advocated in their religion without any consideration of truth or untruth involved. The phrases like 'So far as Bible is concerned, the sun moves round the earth and so far as science is concerned earth moves round the sun ruled the roost.

An advocate of co-existence: A great visionary saint Dayanand could realise in the middle of the 19th century itself the need for the principles of co-existence for the survival of humanity in the world. Today this idea is much talked about but nobody or no nation knows how to follow the principle of co-existence. In the 10th principle of Arya Samaj, Dayanand lays down the very fundamental underlying principles of co-existence. Accordingly, one individual person or nation should be free in abiding by the rules that concern one's own self-interest but an individual person or nation should not be free in abiding by the rules that concern the interests of the entire society or world. Through these lines his message is clear. He is not against individual freedom, but he is against the freedom enjoyed by individual person or nation at the cost of others.

Awareness towards the preservation of Environment: Today the world is facing environmental hazard. The biological life is standing on the verge of extinction from this planet. Due to the depletion of ozone layer and growing pollution, global warming is increasing. Rishi Dayanand emphasised for the preservation of the environment. He was well aware that the human beings through their various activities are polluting the environment. According to him, it is ardent duty of every individual to help preserve the environment. The activities for preserving environment were called by him as *Yajña* or *Agnihotra*. He doesn't want to introduce *Yajña* or *Agnihotra* as some religious tool or activity but as a tool to purify environment as advocated in the Vedas and Gītā. He explains the aim of *Yajña* in the *Ṛgvedādibhāṣya-bhūmikā* as to purify the environment and precipitation of Rain.

An advocate of Education: Rishi Dayanand was the ardent advocate of education to ensure the upliftment of human beings and their real freedom. He laid down the 8th principle of Arya Samaj as: 'We should diffuse knowledge and dissipate ignorance'. According to Romain Rolland, the eighth principle of Arya Samaj - '*to diffuse knowledge and dissipate ignorance*' - has played a great part in the education of India. -----which seeks to resuscitate the energies of the race and to use at the same time the intellectual and technical conquests of the West. Thus Rishi Dayanand was well aware of the fact that the progress of human race was not possible without proper education. Education is the power and strength of an Individual and a nation.

An advocate of Equal Status to women: Today's world is grappling for providing women with the equal status of men. Many women organisations have come up to safeguard the interests of women and to launch the tirade against gender bias and discrimination on the basis of gender. Rishi Dayanand was the first person in the modern history of humankind who placed women at a respectable place, perhaps, at a higher place even than the men. He quotes *Manusmṛti* and observes: *yatra nāryastu pujyante, ramante tatra devatā*, i.e. Gods reside there, where the women are respected.

To sum up it can be observed that Dayanand's contribution of 10 principles of Arya Samaj is not only the contribution to Arya Samaj or Indian society but the contribution to the entire human race for its co-existence and ever existence with friendship and fraternity.

The death of such a stalwart was mourned throughout the country. The news published in various newspapers signalled the contribution of Rishi Dayanand to the Indian society, humankind, cause of education and evil and superstition free society.

Although each and every newspaper mourned the death of this great man, but here I could give quotes from 41 newspapers and magazines due to the courtesy of Prof. Bhawani Lal Bharatiya. He procured all these quotes for me from his personal collection. For this, I am really thankful to Prof. Bharatiya who enabled me to pay my humble tributes to this great man of the present millennia after Mahabharata war by way of editing and organising this work 125 years after his death. These tributes were the last signatures of this visionary man after his mortal remains were consigned to flames at the crematorium of Malusar in Ajmer.

These 41 tributes quoted in this small

treatise are from the newspapers and magazines published in Hindi, Urdu, English, Marathi and Gujarati in various parts of India. We also have some bilingual newspapers which published both in Marathi and English and Gujarati and English. The tributes appeared in these papers have been quoted both in Hindi and English. The tributes appeared in Hindi and Urdu listed in this book from serial 1 to 11, 38 and 41 have been translated by the present writer in English and the English tributes appeared from serial no. 14 to 29 have been translated into Hindi by Prof. Bhawani Lal Bharatiya. Thus this small bunch of tributes to the person of the highest stature of Rishi Dayanand, this globe has ever had since the time of *Mahābhārata* is just like a drop of water into the ocean of Dayanand. The real tributes to him will be paid when his social, academic and spiritual agenda will be redeemed; when his universal and humanitarian ideas will be revealed before the world; when the spiritual, astronomical and astrophysical worth of the Vedas be revealed to the gaze of all; when innocent humanity will get rid of the cobweb of religions; when the truth will be allowed to prevail; when the people will develop scientific outlook; when the entire world be free from different types of superstitions advocated by various religions as well as the science; when the people will come to know about the science behind myth and get rid of myth of science; when the people on the globe will follow the Vedic principle of 'live and help others to live'; when the spirituality will replace religion and science, polity and economy will be governed by spirituality and *dharma*; when discrimination of human beings on the basis of caste, creed, religion, region and race will be abolished.

Rishi Dayanand belonged to the category of Vedic Rishis like Yajñavalkya, Vasiṣṭha and Viśvāmitra etc. so far as his Vedic erudition was concerned. He was far-sighted like Yogiraj Krishna who could visualise real cause of misery and liberation of Bharat. He was a great social thinker who studied Indian society deeply and used his own brain rather relying on someone else's advice to find out the way of India's misery and freedom from foreign yoke. He was just like the sun which shines forth with its own light. His contemporary social reformers and scholars were like that of the moon who tried to illuminate with the help of the light of the sun of foreign ideas and education. According to Rishi Dayanand path of India's freedom passes not from the west, but from India herself. It was not western education that could have helped Indians liberate from the foreign yoke, but it was the Vedic education that could have given them real freedom and made them stand firm on their feet. The freedom earned through swadeshi (indigenous) means is the permanent one, whereas the freedom earned through alien means is temporary and short lived. An elephant is more strong and powerful than the lion, but he is not able to recognise his power due to her small vision, so scares from the lion. Similarly, Indians lost their vision and could not recognise their power and greatness, so they were bowing down before foreigners. Rishi Dayanand was trying to get them realised about their power, so that they may be able to get rid of a foreign yoke. But as opined by several papers while paying their glowing tributes to the Renaissance Rishi that India was unfortunate that Rishi Dayanand passed away shortly.

Vilaspur Samachar observes as under:

> Now a great void has been created. Who will deliver such lectures and who will unravel the truth? Who will dare to bring out the gems delving deep into the ocean of Vedas?

> How will the true meaning of the Vedas be revealed? How will the fraud views about Vedas be encountered now? How can we hope for the reflection of Vedic light in the absence of the sun of Dayanand, the reflector of that light.

Tributes to Swami Dayanand Saraswati

Shocked at the sudden demise of Rishi Dayanand, the Hindi paper Shubh Chintak exclaims:

> Alas! Havens have fallen. The well-wisher of India has passed away. The star of the globe, the resurrector of the Vedas has gone into oblivion. Mountain high personality among human beings has fizzled out. The harbinger of Golden age is no more. Alas! Our master has left us bereaved. A great Yogi, a towering scholar and the messenger of God has deserted us. The Indian flag, the glittering jewel in the crown of India has withered away. The well-wisher of the entire world and the inhabitant of heaven has breathed his last.

Munshi Wazed Ali Saheb, the secretary Anjuman Islamia, Lahore mourns the death of Rishi Dayanand as follows:

> 'O Āryāvartta! Let me cry at your fate. O Āryāvartta my heart sinks when I look at your orphaned condition. I am feeling so sorry at your helplessness. I am feeling so sorry for your piteous condition. . . . .O God were you not happy to see us being brought up in a good manner? Were you not happy to see us move pace to pace with the world? Were you not happy to see us get rid of destructive fetters of superstitions and hypocrisy? Was it not acceptable to you that we are liberated from unnecessary and uncalled for religious bigotry? . . . . Was it not acceptable to you that we remove differences from us (Hindus and Muslims)? Was it not acceptable to you that we understand each other and love each

other? Was it not acceptable to you that we are trained in true religion once more? Was it not acceptable to you that we regain our lost name? Was it not acceptable to you that we learn the true and real religion again and be benefited by the blessings showered by you upon your sons?.... We were innocent, he (Dayanand) used to identify good things for us. We were not able to get up due to our weakness, but he was able to make us rise. We were not able to speak due to lack of knowledge, but he made us speak. We got stuck in the marshy land of superstitions; he used to get us out of superstitions and made us walk on the firm ground of reality. We fettered ourselves with the noose of customs and rituals, he used to liberate us from narrow mindedness. We used to hate our brothers, he used to make us learn to love each other. We curtailed our eyes and did gold plating in our hearts, he used to teach us that for the true religion, outer symbols have no meaning. We considered the wrong customs as good habits, but he proved them to be the bad ones. We lost our essence; he wanted us to regain the same. O God we have driven away from You, but he wanted to bring us into proximity with You. O God You are the best judge of Yourself, why did you separate him from us so soon? Please have pity on us.

The above observations of a Muslim fellow from Lahore are clear cut indications that Muslims were also shocked by the sudden death of Rishi Dayanand. They could realise the fact that Dayanand was guiding everybody on the right path. They were also able to understand his interpretation of religion and

God and his genuine intention of leading the people of all sects on the right path of freedom.

Victoria paper in Sialkot (Present Pakistan) describes the death of Rishi Dayanand no less damaging than the tremors of Central Asia and eruptions of lava on the mountains of Java.

An Urdu paper Oudh Akhbar from Lucknow describes his death as the loss of a greatest Sanskrit Scholar.

Badaun Samachar informs that the shock waves of Dayanand's death have engulfed Russia, China, London, America, Africa and Germany.

Most of the English papers remembered him as an eminent Sanskrit scholar.

Indian Empire, an English paper from Calcutta recalls that Dayanand's vast scholarship, the remarkable power of debate and unimpeachable independence of character will be proudly remembered by his mourning countrymen.

Indian Spectator of Calcutta calls him as one of the pillars of Āryāvartta.

It will not be feasible to quote all the papers here. The readers will find their views in the ensuing pages.

It may be mentioned here that had the Hindus followed Rishi Dayanand, by today India would have been the world leader and guide in all spheres of life. Hindus would have been admired and appreciated by the academic world. Except for Dayanand, there is no alternative for the cultural survival of Hindus. They shall have to come under the umbrella of Dayanand if they want to exit on the globe with glory and dignity and keep their identity alive. The sooner they come, the better it is. Here it may also be pointed out that modern Arya Samajis have also abandoned the path shown by Dayanand. They have become lethargic and greedy. Arya Samaj has a lot of property. Everyone wants to grab some property. They have made Arya Samaj their business and not mission. Arya Samaj is purely an academic institution, but the people at the helm of affairs are doing business instead of academics. That is why Arya Samaj has never been admired and appreciated by the academic world. Arya Samajis are involved in temple constructions, doing Sandhya and Sanskaras alone in the temples. Sometimes, they take out some processions. They are teaching their own folks, they never try to reach out to others about Vedas and Arya Samaj Mission. Every Arya Samaj has its own Sandhya book published and they consider it their great contribution. Most of the Arya Samajs are bringing out petty newspapers often depicting their own photos and criticising others. They are losing the academic fervour. India survived through the vis sc etudes of time due to her academic strength. Academics is the soul of an organisation or a nation. Without academic power and its say into the academic world, Arya Samaj will be a dead body. It is the urgency of time that Arya Samajis should wake up from the sleep and rejuvenate themselves. It is the Arya Samaj only that can make a difference for the better, that can make a history. If Arya Samajis fail this time, Arya Samaj will become the part of history. Arya Samaj has to show to the world that Dayanand is still alive. To keep Dayanand alive will be the real tribute to the Renaissance Rishi and the Scholar Par Excellence.

This book also produces time 9 original photos of Rishi Dayanand sketched at various places. Hope our readers will like this rare legacy of Rishi. Generally, we come across many photos of Rishi Dayanand, but we do not know any historical context associated with them. Here I have made an humble attempt to provide the historical context associated with them. Initially, these photos were made available to me by Prof. Bhawani

Lal Bharatiya, but those photos were not found workable for printing purposes. Finally, I could get some original copies of from Sh. Madhur Ji of Madhur Prakashan Delhi. As such I express my sincere thanks to Madhur Ji for making me available these rare photos of Rishi Dayanand. In fact, we find mention of around 14 original photos of Rishi Dayanand sketched at different places during his lifetime. But we are able to discover only 9 photos and the same are produced here for our esteemed readers.

Dr. Ravi Prakash Arya
114, Akash, DRDO Complex
Lucknow Road, Timarpur, Delhi-110054
Ph. 91 9313033917; 91 11 65188114
vedicscience@rediffmail.com

Tributes Paid by Hindi Papers

1

Hindi Pradeep[1]

Sad News About Swami Dayanand

Hindustan will be called unfortunate as her well-wisher left hurriedly for heavenly abode. Everybody would have mourned the death of Swami Dayanand save few Brahmana cheats devoid of knowledge who are not able to understand the diplomacy of British. Arya Samaj has become armless, the treasure of Sarasvati (Goddess of learning) has been robbed off, the programme of reformation of ruptured society has got a setback. It is only due to this great man that the people from all Varnas in India are able to have access to the Vedas which are the essence of Indian culture and religion. Till date, even the great scholars were not able to pluck out the actual and

---

[1] Hindi Pradeep was a monthly Hindi paper started by Hindi's famous essay writer, editor and prose-write Pt. Balkrishna Bhatt from Sept. 1, 1886. He faced lot of difficulties in bringing this monthly out. So far as the ideology was concerned, Mr. Bhatt was a Paurāṇika, but he supported Swami Dayanand's agenda of social reform and national development.

factual estimate of the Veda. Now many scholars have become curious to delve deep into the ocean of the Vedas and bring out the gems from these sacred texts. In addition to the revival of Vedas, they have left no stone unturned to reform the Hindu society. There is saying in Persian: *kadra mardum baad mardum*, i.e. a man is respected after his death. Now at the sudden demise of this great man, people will realise his greatness and importance. The jewellers with little knowledge about diamond may assess the real diamond for a piece of glass, but we would not fail to appreciate the contribution of Dayanand.

2
'Prerak' Hindi Pradeep, Prayag

Alas! today the sun that caused the lotus of Indian progress to bloom has set. Alas! a good physician who was able to treat the Vedas of all anomalies has fizzled out. Alas! the commander of the ship of the Aryans has gone into oblivion without handing over the charge to the competent person. O' the ocean of true compassion, the showerer of benevolence where have you lost? Having irrigated Bharat land with his knowledge and good preaching O' Short-lived Brahma, why did you introduce your scholarship to the world of uncivilised. Were you not aware that cruel times want to turn Bharat into an irremediable land? That is why it had dispossessed its Brahmans from knowledge and penance and converted them into amorous persons having a lust for money and worldly allurements. Kṣatriyas have been dispossessed of their bravado and knowledge of weaponry (military science). Their bravery and rage have lost in the hoary past. In the company of their ancestors, even the bears and monkeys became valorous fighters who were later regarded as demi-gods. Now the situation has taken a 'U' turn. Their company paralyse even a great warrior to behave like a eunuch. There were times when Acharyas of diplomacy like Maharishi Vasistha were the ideal for the Kṣatriyas, But now the singers and dancers have replaced them. Assessing the futility of time, you (Dayanand) have observed silence but failed to make out whether this cruel time is going to help the redemption of your pledge or not. Now those jackals (so-called scholars) who used to show up themselves in your absence, who went into hiding at your lion-like uproar, and the stomach filling crows (Brahmans who used to grab money from the innocent people in the society) who have become your enemy apprehending the loss of livelihood now will make marry and celebrate your death. There is not an iota of doubt that you did not waste even a single minute for the welfare and upliftment of deprived and downtrodden of this unfortunate country. You could also have enjoyed a luxurious and prosperous life like Mahantas (highest priests) and Mathadhishas (directors of seminaries). You could have also exploited money, minds and bodies of thousands of your blind followers by providing them passports and VISAS for their direct entry into heaven and ensuring them the luxuries of life therein.

Alas! O unbiased, unattached, unselfish,

great educator, a provider of full bloom to the herds of lotuses of love like that of the glittering sun, where did you come stranded in this country of Bharat which is full of mean and satanic ideas.

Alas! O Swami Dayanand! Had you descended on some part of Europe with this spirit of mentor and guide, the ladder of progress and development you were constructing would have seen the light of the day and the countries after countries would have followed suit? Not only they would have enterprise to establish your name and fame, but they would have also transformed your mission into reality and there would have been thousands of branches and sub-branches all through. This would have marred the atmosphere of gaiety among jackals and crows (Pauranic Brahmanas, Christian missionaries and Muslim Maulvis) that have gained momentum at your sad and sudden disappearance from this world. Your ongoing programme of Vedic Interpretation could not have faced a jolt. Now, who will come forward to own this responsibility after your sad and sudden demise? We are well aware that you have defeated the very mission of the God Himself who was determined not to produce a worthy saint to lead this holy land of Bharata Varsha. O line king of Bharat and

Bharati (Indian culture), why did you leave for the heavenly abode immediately leaving this land destitute and bereaved. Did you come to know that superstitions and hypocrisy started getting hold of heaven too that forced you to make your presence feel there just to eliminate these evils thereof? Undoubtedly, you are quite worthy to be the master of Gods. There is also no doubt that the holy saints (Rishis) like you can not stay in the mundane world for a long period.

There are many literary sources to prove this fact. Just as the patient with weak digestion who have lost their appetite are cured by a dextrous physician with proper treatment of sour, salty and hot tastes, similarly you tried to treat the society of its diseases like idolatry, to bring back the shining of the weathered faces of wayward people of the society. This fact is either known to those ancient seers whose cherished wishes you were fulfilling through this endeavour or known to those generous well wishers of this country who could recognise your contribution to the development of the country. As a closing remark, it is disclosed that this author had an opportunity to meet only once to the great man in respect of whom this tribute is being paid. 13 years have passed since I conversed with him in Sanskrit at

Vasukeshwar. Since then he frequented this place many times, but I could not meet him again solely with the view that I did not find myself suitable for his teaching, being involved too much into the mundane world. Now having heard his demise, I have placed on record all the things that must be followed by all those who consider themselves as Aryans. Now I beg pardon from all the gentlemen for my appropriate or inappropriate comments and pray to Almighty to produce one more Dayanand blazing like the sun who can extirpate fundamentalism from Bharat. His purity of faith and pursuit of truth makes us believe that the initiative taken by him may never be stalled.

I have a firm belief that the persons who have been entrusted with this responsibility will carry out their duties amicably. It has always been in the nature of the things that great persons always hand over their legacy to their close followers. For instance, at the twilight hours, the sun moves to his resting place by handing over the programme of elimination of darkness to the god of fire and the god of fire takes rest in the morning resting his faith in the sun. Who knows not this fact that the propagation of true Śāstras and true knowledge and elimination of hypocrisy from Indian society was a mission very dear to Swamiji. He used to air these ideas in his speeches from time to time. Thus the man and mission of Swamiji were well known to everybody. And if this mission is carried out with true spirit, this will lead to the happy end. Moreover, if this mission of Swamiji is headed by His Highness Maharana of Udaipur himself, then this mission will certainly be awarded and will see its successful culmination.

3
Bharat Bandhu[2]

We were shocked to know that His Holiness Dayanand Sarasvati left for the heavenly abode on Oct. 30, 1983, i.e. Amavasya of Kartika month of Vikram Saṁvat 1940. The vacuum created by the sudden demise of a scholar like Swami Dayanand is a very unfateful event in the history of India. We were not able to bear the shock of the death of Bal Shastri. Destined as if we are to face shock after shock. Now we face a desideratum of a scholar in India who is courageous, intelligent, diligent, orator, proficient in all Śāstras like that of Swami Dayanand. It was Swamiji who made the Christians and Muslims realise that Arya religion is the oldest and best of all religions of the world. It has been witnessed that the high profile Maulvis who excelled in Arabic and Persian remained dumbfounded before the towering scholarship of Swami Dayanand. It may not be out of context to mention here that Swami Ji was a person of ready wit.

---

[2] This weekly news paper started publishing in 1886 from Aligarh. Totaram Verma, a litterateur Bharatendu age was its editor. This continued to be published till 1894.

Whenever a question was posed to him, he replied the same rationally corroborating with evidence. We did never meet a prolific speaker and scholar like him.

He also made the British rulers realise that Aryan religion is superior to theirs. This fact was proved by him during his academic debates with Christian fathers. He was held in high esteem even in the western countries. Till date, no Indian scholar could make his reverend place in western countries like him. His commentary on Vedas is unparalleled in the history of India. Although his commentary at some places stands in sharp contrast to our ancient commentators, still we appreciate it, because that is the evidence of his erudition. Under the circumstances, we Indians must hold Dayanand as one of the glittering jewels of Bharat Land. However, the time is powerful enough to engulf the great stalwart like him.

4
Shubh Chintak[3]

The above-cited paper gives glowing tributes to Rishi Dayanand in a poetical style. The Hindi poem was composed in Shikharini Metre. Hereunder is rendered the brief summary of the poem:

Alas! Havens have fallen. The well-wisher of India has passed away. The star of the globe, the resurrector of the Vedas has gone into oblivion. Mountain high personality among human beings has fizzled out. The harbinger of Golden age is no more. Alas! Our master has left us bereaved. A great Yogi, a towering scholar and the messenger of God has deserted us. The Indian flag, the glittering jewel in the crown of India has withered away. The well-wisher of the entire world and the inhabitant of heaven has breathed his last. Our master having consecrated the galaxy of scholars has moved away. The leader of the world, the seer of the seers has shifted to heavens. Alas! The star of our hearts has disappeared. The leader who was leading us across the ocean of darkness has sunk himself in the ocean of Almighty.

[3] This was a monthly paper published from Shahjahanpur in 1883.

Alas! Our master has flown to the final destination. Swami Ji left his mission incomplete. He advocated the Vedic views in Jodhpur. He taught Vedas to the king of Jodhpur, thus setting a good tradition of Vedic teaching and learning in the royal families. All hypocrite Brahmanas disappeared from the scene just like stars in the night sky disappear in Moonlight. The celebrated Swami Ji has passed away. The Brahmanas poisoned Swamiji when they heard him exposing the Vedic truths, as their lively-hood was at stake. When these perverted Brahmanas found themselves deprived of their lively-hood, they committed the crime against humanity and Swami Ji fell a prey to their conspiracy. He went to Mount Abu for the recovery of his health. When his health began to deteriorate further he returned to Ajmer. The poison burnt down the whole body and Swamiji suffered from unbearable pain. On the auspicious day of Diwali, Swami Ji left his mortal remains. It was 1940 of Vikrama era and 1883 of Christian era when Swamiji left for heavenly abode. He could not complete his interpretations of the Vedas since he failed to recover from the effect of poison. He left for heavenly abode with his desire to complete his commentary of all the four Vedas unfulfilled. His untimely death rendered his mission incomplete. Swami Ji left having uttered the word, 'Let O' God your will be fulfilled!'. The trees planted by me should be irrigated with the nectar of love so that after their growth these trees may laden with fruits and feed the whole world. People should have firm faith in Vedas, this was only the will of Swami Ji at the time of his death. Let us pray to God to fulfil the will of emancipated Swami Ji.

5

Vilaspur Samachar[4]

In Vilaspur Samachar, a poetical tribute appeared written by Ram Prakash. The English translation of tribute is rendered hereunder.

On 30th Oct. 1883 (*Kartika Amavasya* of Vikram *Saṁvat* 1940) on the day of Tuesday, every nook and corner of the country were lightened with the Deepas of Diwali. Swami Dayanand having meditated and prayed to the Almighty God at the time of Sandhya escorted by the air-vehicle of devas left for the abode which was already occupied by the Vedic Rishis like Vamadeva and Vyasa.

Now a great void has been created. Who will deliver such lectures and who will unravel the truth? Who will dare to bring out the gems delving deep into the ocean of Vedas?

How will the true meaning of the Vedas be revealed? How will the fraud views about Vedas be encountered now? How can we hope for the reflection of Vedic light in the absence of the sun of Dayanand, the reflector of that light?

---

[4] This paper published from Vilaspur, Madhyapradesh. Today Vilaspur is in Chhatisgarh.

O Dayanand! blessed, are you? Having achieved a son like you, the world feels highly graced. You have broken all the ties of relationship and left this Bharat destitute. Have mercy on this country which is reeling under misery and poverty and finds no way to come out of plight and depravity. The whole Āryāvartta is praying to the Almighty to grant strength and perseverance to bear this great loss. This has attributed a great pain to the world, even the stone would melt down having heard it what to say about the human beings.

For the last two thousand years, I (Aryavartta) was suffering greatly and was not able to offer my services to my countrymen. Having mercy on me O God, you blessed me with a virtuous son Dayanand Sarasvati who was determined to eliminate my sufferings. Leaving aside selfish motives, only he turned towards my (Aryavartta's) welfare. He was one of my jewels and the best devotee of yours O God. You have taken the only custodian of mine away. There is no country in the world so unfortunate as me. What is my mistake O Almighty! for which you are punishing me with sufferings after sufferings? I was not able to recover from the shock of the death of Rama, Krishna and Shankara, the death of Dayanand has come as a final death blow. Having achieved Dayanand, I was able to recover from the shock of Rama, Krishna and Shankara. I was really blessed to find a blessed son in Dayanand whose glory was encompassing the entire globe. He came as your incarnation. The land of Gujrat also became blessed with his birth. Virjananda was also blessed finding in him a great disciple. He revived the lost Vedas along with their true intent. He made the people happy. He prevailed upon the society in all the four directions. He founded the society of Arya (noble and civilised men). At this precarious juncture, he carried out such programmes that were the dire needs of the hour. He engaged in my (Aryavartta's) well being by all means but now left me bereaved. I do not find even a single Arya in the world who is not bewailing your son's death O God. He has thrown me into the den of deep shock, after all, no one can escape the destiny. O God! take care of me. I pray to you with both hands folded. Now I am in your custody. You have orphaned me. It is You who can de-orphan me. Where else can I go leaving your shelter? Protect me O God. Protect me. I humbly pray to you. All Aryas can pray to God to grant a caretaker to Bharat land. Bharat is crying miserably. Listen to our humble request O God. You are the custodian of the whole world, kindly guide us where to go now.

6
Sajjan Kirti Sudhakara[5]

Sajjan Kirti Sudhakar was the newspaper of Udayapur state. The highest administrative body of Uadayapur State paid tributes to Swami Dayanand. Maharana of Udaipur expressed his heartfelt condolences at the sudden and sad demise of Swami Dayanand Sarasvati. These tributes published in Sajjan Kirti Sudhakara in the form of a poem written in Avadhi style of Hindi language. The following is the English translation.

I consider him the renaissance leader of the whole Āryāvartta, who was able to exterminate hypocrisy. He had the power of a lion who was able to uproot the anti-Vedic ideology and superstitions from the Indian society. I think the expert of six Śāstras, resurrector of the Vedas, and the visionary son (sun) has set. I think Dayanand was a divine Pārijata tree of heaven who has fallen

---

[5] Sajjan Kirti Sudhakar was the Gazette of Udaypur, Mewar state. Its publication started in 1949. By that time Maharana Sajjan Singh was the ruler of Mewar. This name to the paper was given by Swami Dayanand himself. This paper published historical and social matter in addition to the Govt. orders and news.

now. The source of Yoga, the advocate of true sciences in Vedas has left for the heavenly abode. The satanic forces that have strayed from the right path, the follower of leftist ideas, animal killers have the heyday now. Jai Karan states that the expounder of the duties of the four Varnas has achieved salvation. The publisher of three Vedas, the propagator of good ideas, and the speaker of truth has left this earth destitute. He differentiated between good and bad, truth and false, water and milk, authentic and inauthentic texts. Had he not descended upon the earth, the gems of the Vedas would have been lying hidden and unattended by the scholars. The poet of poets Shyamal Das opines that the scholar who let us know that Vedas are the basis of the six Śāstras has left for heavenly abode. Alas! Today the interest of Aryas has been wiped out by the flow of river whose bridge has ripped apart.

7
Benaras Press[6]

This tribute was also paid in the poetic form by Kedar Sharma, the editor of the Benaras press. The English Translation of the same is rendered hereunder:

'Time is great. No one can escape it. The valiant heroes like Arjuna, Karna, Drona, Kuntibhoja, Parikshit, Raghu, Pandu, all had to surrender at last. Similarly the preacher of Vedas, Dayanand Sarasvati could also not escape the hazards of time.

O Dayanand Sarasvati, the jewel of Gurjar country, why did you leave your mortal remains so soon? Did the idol worship forced you to leave for heaven? Or you reached the court of Indra just to remind him of the harms of idolatry. Or you wanted to win over the heavens after being victorious on the earth. Or you went to Brahma just to clarify few doubts about the meaning of Vedas. O Dayanand

---

[6] This was the first Hindi paper to be published from Benaras in 1845. In fact it was a Urdu paper which used to be published in Devanagari Script. Its publisher and owner was Raja Shivprasad Sitarehind who was the supporter of Urdu language. This paper was edited by Govind Raghunath Thate, a Marathi person.

Sarasvati! This country cannot afford to forget your contribution towards her progress. Now the Pandits have become free to give a false interpretation of Dharmaśāstras. They would not distinguish between true and false and would lay a trap for the innocents. You opened up so many schools and installed Maharana Sajjan Singh as the chairperson of Propakarini Sabha. No one can appreciate the contribution of Swami Ji as it was appreciated by His highness, Sajjan Singh. So long as the ship of Bharat land continues to sink, Swami Ji thundered like that of a lion and all jackals got scared of his thunder. He trounced all pretty scholars and earned a lot of name and fame. How many scholars challenged him in debates, but he as the treasure house of Sarasvati never gave in. He immediately appreciated the good views and set aside the hypocritical ideas. All gentlemen in India are making laudatory comments about him every day.

One more glowing tribute was given in the form of kavitta (one of the forms of poetry). The same may be recalled as under:

Swami Ji visited all the cities located in all the four directions of the country and challenged the Pandits for the debates. All the Pandits were defeated in the debates. He received tremendous applause in the entire country. This earth can never have a parallel to Swami Ji who excelled in all the 14 arts of knowledge and who was a great exponent of the Vedas.

Tributes Paid by Urdu papers
8
Deshopakarak[7]

As soon as the telegraphic message of the sudden demise of Swami Ji Maharaj was received in Multan, on Oct. 13, 1883, the notice of public mourning was circulated immediately. In connection with the mourning, a huge crowd assembled in the premises of Arya Samaj. In addition to the leaders of Arya Samaj, fairly large number of the people representing Hindus, Muslims and Christians also poured in. During the condolence assembly, a businessman who was not the member of Arya Samaj came forward to express his heartfelt condolences at the sudden demise of the leader of the age. His speech was followed by the speeches of Lal Chand Sirkar and Kashi Prasad, the vice president. Their speeches made everyone present in the assembly burst into tears. Similar such assemblies were held there time and again. Hindus and Muslims equally participated into those assemblies and felt bereaved. Let us reproduce here a sample of

---

[7] Lala Laj Pat Rai started its publication from Lahore in January 1883.

written speeches delivered by Munshi Wazed Ali Saheb, the secretary Anjuman Islamia at one of such occasions. The speech is reproduced here as it is. It goes like this:

'O Āryāvartta! Let me cry at your fate. O Āryāvartta my heart sinks when I look at your orphaned condition. I am feeling so sorry at your helplessness. I am feeling so sorry for your pity condition. How quickly the eyes of your beloved one have closed. O God was you not happy to see us being brought up in a good manner? Were you not happy to see us move pace to pace with the world? Were you not happy to see us get rid of destructive fetters of superstitions and hypocrisy? Was it not acceptable to you that we are liberated from unnecessary and uncalled for religious bigotry? Was it not acceptable to you that we are liberated from dastardly social customs? Was it not acceptable to you that we remove differences from us (Hindus and Muslims)? Was it not acceptable to you that we understand each other and love each other? Was it not acceptable to you that we are trained in true religion once more? Was it not acceptable to you that we regain our lost name? Was it not acceptable to you that we learn the true and real religion again and be benefited by the blessings showered by you upon your sons? Everything was going as intended and desired by you. Then why did you strip us off our affectionate thing? That is to say, why did you summon so soon on Oct. 30, at 6 PM our friend and well-wisher Swami Dayanand Sarasvati who used to teach us all the good things. Although the darkness of Amavasya has been dispelled by the light of lamps lit on the occasion of Diwali, but the real sun has gone into oblivion. We were innocent, he used to identify good things for us. We were not able to get up due to our weakness, but he was able to make us rise. We were not able to speak due to lack of knowledge, but he made us speak. We got stuck in the marshy land of superstitions; he used to get us out of superstitions and made us walk on the firm ground of reality. We fettered ourselves with the noose of customs and rituals, he used to liberate us from narrow mindedness. We used to hate our brothers, he used to make us learn to love each other. We curtailed our eyes and did gold plating in our hearts, he used to teach us that for the true religion, outer symbols have no meaning. We considered the wrong customs as good habits, but he proved them to be the bad ones. We lost our essence; he wanted us to regain the same. O God we have driven away from You, but he wanted us to be in proximity to You. O God You are the best judge of Yourself, why did you separate him from us so soon? Please have pity on us.

9
Victoria Paper[8]

The sudden demise of Swami Dayanand is no less damaging than the tremors of Central Asia and eruptions of lava on the mountains of Java. The life of such a stalwart of Sanskrit has its impact on the lives of millions, and the death of such a towering personality who was associated with a religion which was writ large in Hindostan must have been more shocking than the death of millions. The astrologers who considered red horizons at the twilight hours as bad omen foretelling some catastrophe were proved right because there cannot be a bigger catastrophe than this one for the Hindu race. This may be called as unfortunate for Hindus because a personality like Swami Saheb has fizzled out of their gaze so soon. The insistence of Swami Saheb that Hindus or Aryas should aware of the principles and laws of their religion and they should know the teachings of the Vedas so that they may shape their fortune accordingly, was such an attempt as would have opened the

---
[8] This paper was named after the queen Victoria. It was published in Urdu from Syalkot located presently in Pakistan.

gates of relief to the Hindus and they would be their own mentors. We are sorry to say that our entire hopes have dashed to grounds. Who has not died? Who will not die? But the death of such a personality who descended on the earth to guide the humanity (especially Hindus) to the right path is really a shocking for Hindus.

Swami Dayanand was not a Saṁnyāsī for the namesake, but he was a Saṁnyāsī in the real sense of terms. He had no vested interests or selfish motives. Selflessness is not a simple thing, but the greatest quality blessed by God to a few chosen ones. Everybody tries to project himself/herself as taintless and clean. The elephant has two types of tasks, one for show and another for eating. During this month of Vaishakh, when I was on my visit to Udayapur, I heard it from the mouth of the responsible persons that Swami Saheb was offered Rs. 2000.00 by the king's court of Udayapur, but Swami Saheb accepted for himself only the travelling expenses, rest of the money was donated by him to the Propakarini Sabha which was supposed to carry out his mission after his death under the President-ship of His Highness Maharana Udayapur. The sole objective of this gesture was, as I was given to understand by the reliable sources, to propagate his mission in public and to translate the Vedas. Who can claim that this objective of Swami Saheb can be redeemed easily? A human being is not stable. Every day his ideas change. It is not easy to tread the path of truth. Let us pray to God to bless everybody to follow the path of truth like that of Swami Ji. We know that the president of this assembly is the learned ruler whose Riyasat has a prominent place in Rajasthan and by the grace of God he himself has spent a lot of money to fund the activities of Sabha, but the need is that branches of Sabha be established in every district of this country which should work towards the redemption of Swami Ji's objectives.

The membership of this Sabha is increased spectacularly. A Hindu who can donate two annas (one anna is equal to six paise) monthly be allowed to be the member of this Sabha, so that a proper infrastructure for making public true principles of Hinduism and true intent of Vedas as per Swami Ji's interpretations be prepared and Hindus can benefit themselves with the ideas and knowledge of Swami Ji. Though Swami Ji has passed away, yet the Hindus should constantly feel the presence of Swami Ji through his programmes undertaken everywhere in India. The persons who had basic differences of ideas from Swami Saheb or who were biased because of their selfish motives had deprived themselves of the company of Swami Saheb. Now also they will find it difficult to accept this clarion call. However, the persons who were aware of the ground realities and who could understand Swami Ji's selfless pious mission, who could find salvation through Swami Ji's ideas, who could see their progress and development in the genuine efforts put up by Swamiji, or who could make out the objective behind his plain speaks, who could understand the actual mission of Swami Ji or the progress and advancement plan dreamt by Swami Ji for Hindus, they cannot find fault with this appeal of mine. They will also be happy to found a memorial of Swami Ji. They will certainly cry and complain to the Almighty as to why He has taken Dayanand Sarasvati into hiding. Having heard the news of sudden demise of Swami Ji, we are not able to hold our tears back, our heart starts sinking. Under the circumstances, no way out is seen but simply to quote an Urdu poet:

> The octogenarian people usually observe that there is no home left where the death has not knocked the doors.

10
Arya Samachar[9]

Whose death has taken our lives? Everybody is bewailing. Let me know who has died?

As soon as the shocking news reached the city through a telegraphic message that Swami Ji, the proud of the country, a towering scholar and a social reformer of the first order has left this mundane world for the heavenly abode on Oct. 30, 1883, the eyes burst into tears, people become dumbfounded and there was numbness everywhere. Shock waves and uneasiness prevailed through length and breadth of this country. People were becoming unconscious. Although living physically, yet their condition was worse than the dead body. Having heard this news, people were not able to rise from their beds.

Further tributes were paid by the way of an Urdu Nazam (poem) which can be translated

---

[9] This was the first Urdu paper of Arya Samaj which was published weekly from Meerut. Its initial issues were edited by Babu Kalyan Rai. Later on its editing work was started by Andolal, the secretary of Meerut Arya Samaj.

as under:

Yesterday we came to know that he (Dayanand Sarasvati) was not able to leave his bed (due to weakness), today he became so strong that he left this world.

This Nazam was followed by a Nauha (a style of Urdu poetry) which may be read as under:

Today everybody is under shock and distressed. The sorrowful cries are all around. Every Hindu house has bereaved. Tears are flowing down all eyes. Some are beating their chests, others are hitting their heads against walls. This news appeared as a headline in each and every newspaper. Smoke has replaced the fire of *Agnihotra*. Ear rending cries have replaced the reverberations of mantras. Alas! Swami Ji has left this world, now there is no reason for not crying. The crown of the country has tumbled down. The signature of Hindus has been obliterated. The fate of India has taken a 'U' turn. Although the days of progress were ahead, but the regression has set off. India's sky was overcast with the clouds of progress, but the clouds have torn apart before it rained. All our hopes were founded upon him, but the very foundation has dashed to the ground. Stars have left twinkling in the night owing to the great vacuum created by the death of this great personality. He was able to row the boat of knowledge up to the brink, but the same has slipped back into waters. We were about to settle down, but the untimely death of Swamiji has de-settled everything. The separation of Swami Ji has given a great set back to our existence. Everybody is bewailing due to this unprecedented happening. We are unable to control our cries, as our hearts are burning. We were not at all aware that you will leave us in between. The entire world has got stunned and has worn a deserted look. We want to come to you, let us know about your address. You should have made us your accompanist, now we don't see any place worth leaving the earth. Why did you leave us bereaved? Why did you turn a blind eye to us who are crying in helplessness? Now, who will bring us out of tragedy? Now, who will awake us from slumber? Who will impart knowledge to us? Who will awaken us? Who will liberate us from the noose of Pauranikas? Who will protect us from the network of hypocrites? Who will boost our morale and courage and who will enthuse life to the dead? Who will teach us the formulae of progress and advancement? Who will push the sinking boat ashore? Who will make an exposition of Dharma, Artha, Kama and Moksha? Who will fetch us Rishihood? Who will administer Guru mantra to us? Who will teach Veda mantras now? Who will lead us to the path of liberation? Who will teach us chit chat on Vedas? Who will teach us the method and advantages of *Yajña*? Who will bring us out of the fatwa of kafir hood and procure the old name Arya instead of Hindu? Who will make us realise the true meaning of '*so'ham*' (God is within you) and '*tattvamsi*' (Thou are the part of God)? Who will give us freedom? Who explains *Śāstras* to us? Who will interpret *Śrutis* to us? Who will tell us the true meaning of *Dharma*? Who will unravel the meaning of Sutras to us? Who will teach us the practice of *yoga*? Who will tell us the actual procedure of worshipping God? It is easy to acquire the rulership of the whole world, but it is quite difficult to get a Guru like you? Now nobody can come for our safeguard from miseries and problems. Nobody can bless and encourage us to fight out the evils from society. Nobody can register his/her protest in the matter of cow slaughter with Government. It is possible to search a miracle man who can dare troubles and turbulence, but it is quite impossible to search a person who owes a responsibility to mitigate all problems. It is possible for someone to take a tour to all places for propagating *Dharma*, but it is quite impossible to find a scholar who can interpret Vedas. There cannot be any substitute for Swami Ji. The whole world is sinking under shock. There can be no end of crises and there can be no limit of tears. Nobody can ever recover from this shock. We are destined to cry till the end of life. More we try to hush up the fire of our hearts with the help of tears, more it flares up. His memories have imprinted on the hearts of every man, how can they be obliterated. Or the death is imminent, nobody can escape it. How long we shall carry on this unbearable shock. Better to recover from this shock immediately. The best way to pay tributes to Swami Ji is to carry out the agenda of the Vedic mission. Let us pray to almighty to bless the mother earth to have a glorious son like Dayanand again.

11

Badaun Samachar[10]

Presently everybody has swayed by the shock wave of the death of Swamiji. This shock wave has engulfed Russia, China, London, America, Africa and German. The festival of lights (Diwali) has been darkened by this shocking news. Just to come out of melancholy, I tried to take a stroll towards the railway station. A friend of mine happened to meet me on the way. He rushed to me and holding my hands in his hands uttered, 'Do you know something?' Where are you going? Today a telegraphic message has been received from Ajmer. Maharaj has passed away, i.e. Swami Ji is no more. He was known for his brilliant scholarship in the entire world. He was able to bring about a sea change in the country through his preaching and teachings. He really consisted of himself both *Daya* (compassion) and *Ananda* (bliss), as his name Dayanand suggests. Muslims, Christians, Pauranikas, Persians, Jains,

---

[10] This was an Urdu paper published from Badaun.

Chinese, Zoroastrians - nobody could challenge him in the matter of Vedas. Today he left us bereaved and achieved salvation.

Having heard these utterances from the friend, I was shocked and fell down on the earth. Under the circumstances, I found it difficult to live up to Dharma. I was so shocked, that if I start describing my shock with the help of a stick of sealing wax, it can raise into an edifice of an office. My body became numb. There was sensation all through. The life was about to abandon my body. I cannot narrate the condition I underwent. I pray to God not to allow even my enemies to undergo such a shock. When I was not able to control myself anyhow, I complained to almighty himself, 'For what fault of mine, I was punished by You. You could not see our progress. O God You are least frightened that You have gathered here jackals. You could have made 10-20 Popes as Your target than Swami Ji. We have always seen you in opposite direction. Had you taken some more time, heavens were not going to fall, O Perpetrator of shock. You stalled the programme of Vedic commentary. I have only curses for You. O cruel hearted one! have patience. Close this bloody chapter now. In the 1940th year of Vikrama, when the sun was setting, Swami Ji's sunset in forever with the following prayer to Almighty.

'This is Your will. This is Your will. Let it be fulfilled.'

12
Oudh Akhbar[11]

Lucknow, November 8

Although Swami Dayanand Saraswati's views did not meet with general approval, yet the measures taken by him for reforming the Hindu religion will be long remembered. There is no doubt India has lost in him one of her greatest Sanskrit scholars.

---

[11] This was a daily Urdu paper published from Lucknow.

13
The Koh-e-Nur[12] and
The Akhbar-e-Aam

November 3

Suggest that a monument is raised in honour of Swami Dayanand, and to mark the gratitude of his admirers for his just and righteous admonitions.

Note: The Hindustani, the Reformer of Lahore, the Naseem-e-Hind of Fatehpur, the Dubdaba-e-Kesari of Bareilly also expressed great sorrow at the death of the Pandit Dayanand Saraswati.

---

[12] This was a daily Urdu paper published from Lahore. It was popular paper of Munshi Harsukhrai Bhatanagar. Bhatanagar was the main person to invite Swami ji to Punjab.

Tributes paid by English Papers

14
Hindu Observer[13]

Madras, November 8

He was a renowned Sanskrit scholar and an earnest worker in the sphere of reformation. His death is a loss to the country.

---

[13] An English weekly published from Madras.

15

The Thinker[14]

Madras, November 11

We are sorry to hear the death of an eminent Sanskrit scholar, Swamiji Dayanand Saraswati.

We send our hearty words of condolence to his personal friends and followers to whom the news of his death would, no doubt, cause a pang in their heart.

---

[14] This was an English weekly published from Madras.

16
The Bengalee[15]
(Calcutta, November 3)

PANDIT DAYANANDA must be regarded as a religious teacher of no ordinary eminence. We may differ from his religious views; we may not accept his interpretation of the Vedas, but he stands forth as a religious teacher of surpassing power and earnestness. He was a yogi, an ascetic who had abjured the world, but he was gifted with a practical sagacity which few men of the world could pretend to possess. His death is not only an irreparable loss to the religious community of which he was the life and soul, but it is a loss to his countrymen at large, who will always be proud of his learning and cherish his memory with affectionate gratitude.

---

[15] This paper was edited by the famous national leader and patriot Surendra Nath Banerjee. He had also been the member of the council of Viceroy and the president of Indian National congress.

17
Indian Empire[16]

Calcutta, November 4.

It is our painful duty to record the death of Swami Dayanand Saraswati, the distinguished founder of the Arya Samaj, and the foremost of Hindu reformers of his generation. This melancholy event took place at Ajmer on Tuesday last. His vast scholarship, remarkable powers of debate and unimpeachable independence of character will be proudly remembered by his mourning countrymen.

---

[16] English weekly published from Calcutta.

18
Indian Chronicle[17]

Bankipur, November 5

A profound Sanskrit scholar and deeply versed in all the love of Aryan philosophy, an eloquent speaker, and extremely courteous in his manners, he had all the qualifications of a great religious teacher; and indeed his organisation, the Arya Samaj, as a means of religious reformation, is no ephemeral character. It will certainly have a voice in deciding the spiritual future of India. The chief aim of Dayanand Saraswati was to restore the pristine purity of the Hindu religion and clear it of the heaps of esoteric dross under which latter day Brahmanic divines have succeeded in interring it.

---

[17] This was an English weekly published from Bankipur Patna. It may be pointed out here that in those days Bengal and Bihar were one state.

19
Bengal Public Opinion[18]

Calcutta, November 3

Pandit Dayanand's death will cast a gloom over the whole of educated Hindu-dom. He was an ornament to our country; pride to our nation. Whatever might be his errors of judgement, that he was a man of genius few will deny. The Arya Samaj has lost in him a leader whose place they will never again be able to fill up.

---

[18] An English weekly published from Calcutta.

20
Hindoo Patriot[19]

Calcutta, November 5

We are sorry to record the death of two great Sanskritists of India, Pandit Dayanand Saraswati and Pandit Loharam Shirorutna. The first was a most eminent Vedantist (Vedic scholar). He, however, used to give new interpretations to Vedic texts, which did not often tally with those current among orthodox Pandits. He used to speak in Sanskrit and the flow he commanded in that dead language was wonderful. He was the founder of the Arya Samaj. Pandit Loharam was an eminent grammarian.

---

[19] This paper was published in the sixth decade of the 19th century. Its publication was associated with Keshav Chandra Sen, the prominent leader of Brahmo Samaj.

21

The Liberal[20]

Calcutta November 11

Whatever the nature of his religion might be, Pandit Dayanand Saraswati deserved our sympathy and commanded our admiration. Though his mind was not imbued with the truths of Western science, he entertained enlightened views and ideas, foreign to the education he had received, but which seemed to evolve out of his own inner consciousness. May his soul rest in peace.

---

[20] An English weekly published from Calcutta.

22
Indian Messenger[21]

Calcutta, November 11

Barring some peculiarities of doctrine, which, however, were secondary, there never breathed a more sincere hater of the systems of idolatry and priest craft of this country than this remarkable man, and none ever opposed them with such intrepid courage and perseverance. With many of his ideas yet unfulfilled, and his life-work yet unfinished, this true servant of God must have felt the approach of death to be rather sudden and untimely, and his last prayer was the pious resignation of his noble mission to the will of Him; who had called him to the field. May the spirit of this prayer inspire all our actions!

---

[21] This was a weekly paper published in English from Calcutta.

23

The Arya Magazine[22]

November 1883, p. 199

On the very eve of our going to press we have received an intelligence that has shocked every nerve within us. the event reported is the death of our most revered Swamiji Dayanand Saraswati that took place at Ajmer on the evening of the 30th October. His loss we feel, as every true Arya and well-wisher of India should feel a personal and national calamity. His death to the country is a loss which can never be replaced. He was an incarnation of all the virtues that a man can possess; so deep in Vedic lore as to persuade one almost to a belief that he was, though in another body, one of the four Rishis to whom Vedas in the beginning of the world were revealed; a true and devoted patriot of his country, a perfect Yogi for whom a long stay on this lower world, which is unsuited for higher spirits, could not be tolerated by Heaven. Many days before his death, the

---

[22] Ratnachand Beri started the editing and publication of this English monthly from Saidmitha Bazar of Lahore. This paper published the news of sad demise of Swami Dayanand with a black boarder along with the reports of other papers that covered the death of Swamiji.

rising and setting of the sun were preceded and followed by a green, pale and red cloud of light that remained visible at Madras, Deccan and Punjab for hours together for several days successively as if the sun itself were in deep mourning for the departure of the great spirit from its dominion. When the soul of Swamiji left the body, every Hindu house in India was illuminated on account of Diwali festival, and the lights were kept burning all through the night, and the Bhagats - devotees-both male and female, kept themselves awake and engaged in their devotion.

Full particulars of the event will be published as soon as they are communicated to us by the Arya Samaj Ajmer.

24
The Theosophist[23]
Madras, 1883

A master spirit has passed away from India. Pandit Dayanand Saraswati, the founder and supreme chief of the Arya Samaj of Aryavartta, is gone; the irrepressible, energetic reformer, whose mighty voice and passionate eloquence for the last few years raised thousands of people in India from lethargic indifference and stupor into active patriotism, is no more. He passed out of this plane of strife and suffering into a higher and more perfect state of being.

A special telegram from Ajmer brought to the many Samajes the melancholy news that their master Swami Dayanand Saraswati breathed his last at 6 P.M. on 30th October.

De mortuis nil nist bonum.

All our differences have been burnt with the body and with its now sacred ashes they are forever scattered to the four winds. We remember only the grand virtues and noble qualities of our former colleague, teacher and late antagonist. We bear in mind but his life-

---

[23] This was a monthly Journal of Theosophical society of Madras.

long devotion to the cause of Aryan regeneration; his ardent love for the grand philosophy of his forefathers; his relentless, untiring zeal in the work of the projected social and religious reforms; and it is with unfeigned sorrow that we now hasten to join the ranks of his many mourners. In him, India has lost one of her noblest sons. A patriot in the true sense of the word, Swami Dayanand laboured from his earliest years for the recovery of the lost treasures of Indian intellect. His zeal for. the reformation of his motherland was exceeded only by his unbounded learning. Whatever might be said as to his interpretation of the sacred writings, there can be but one opinion as to his knowledge of Sanskrit and the impetus to the study of both received at his hands. There are few towns and but one province we believe-namely, Madras-that Pandit Dayanand did not visit in furtherance of his missionary work, and fewer still where he has not left the impression of his remarkable mind behind him. He threw, as it were, a bombshell in the midst of the stagnant masses of degenerated Hinduism, and fired with love for the teachings of the Rishis and Vedic learning the hearts of all who were drawn within the influence of his eloquent oratory. Certainly, there was no better or grander orator in Hindi and Sanskrit than Swami Dayanand throughout the length and breadth of this land.

As soon as the sad rumour was confirmed, Colonel Olcott, who was then at Kanpur, paid a public tribute to the Swami's memory. He said that whatever might have been our rights or wrongs in the controversy, and whatever other pundits or orientalists could say against the Swami, there was room for no two opinions as to his energetic patriotism or of the nationalising influence exerted upon his followers. In Pandit Dayanand Saraswati there was a total absence of anything like degrading sycophancy and toadyism towards foreigners from interested motives. At Bara Banki, Lucknow our President repeated the same ideas to an immense audience in the Palace-Ground (Kaiser-bag) of the ex-king of Oudh, and the sentiment was warmly acknowledged.

Truly, however heretical and blasphemous might have appeared his religious radicalism in the sight of old orthodox Brahminism, still his teachings and the Vedic doctrines propagated by him were a thousand times more consonant with *Śruti* and even *Smṛti* than the doctrines taught by all other native Samajes put together. If he merged the old idols into One living Being, Iśwara, as being only the attributes and powers of the latter, he yet had never attempted the folly of forcing down the throats of his followers the hideous compound of a Durga. Moses, Christ-and-Koran, and Buddha-Chaitanya mixture of the modern reformers. The 'Arya Samaj' rites make certainly the nearest approach to the real Vedic national religion. And now, on the death of Swamiji, there is no one we know of - in India capable of taking his place. The Arya Samajes, as far as we could ascertain, are all conducted by men who can as little fill the vacant place as a cardboard tree of a dramatical stage can become a substitute for the strong cedar, the king of the Himalayan forests. Loving old Aryavartta, as we do, for its own sake, it is ...with sincereness and fear, and with a deep sense of sympathy for bereaved India, that we say again that the death of Pandit Dayanand Saraswati is an irreparable loss to the whole country. At the present chaotic stage of it's reformatory progress, it is simply a national calamity!

In connection with the above sad event, we may take this opportunity to make a few remarks in answer to a certain surprise expressed by several correspondents. They are at a loss to realise, they state, that a yogi credited with some psychological powers, such as Swamiji Dayanand, was unable to foresee the great loss his death would cause to India; was he then no Yogi, no 'Brahma Rishi' ..as the organization of the Lahore Samaj called him, that he knew it not. To this, we answer that we can swear 'that he had foreseen his death, and so far back as two years ago. Two copies of his Will sent by him at the time to Colonel Olcott and to the editor of this Magazine respectively - both of which are preserved by us as a memorial of his by-gone friendship are a good proof of it.

He told us repeatedly at Meerut he would never see 1883. But even had he not foreseen his death, we do not see what bearing it can have upon the Yogi powers of the defunct. The greatest adepts living are but mortal men after and sooner or later have to die. No adept is proof against accident unless he uses selfishly his acquired powers. For, unless he is constantly watching over his own personality and cares little for the rest of mankind, he is as liable to fall a victim to disease and death as any other man. The childish, not to say absurd, ideas about yogis, and their supernatural powers-whereas they are at best but superhuman that we often find current among our own Theosophists, and the superstitious and grotesque tales narrated of these holy personages among that class of Hindus which, being more orthodox than educated, derives all its ideas from the dead-letter traditions of the *Purāṇas* and *Śāstras*, have very little to do with sober truth. An adept or *Rajayogī* (we now speak of the real not the fictitious ones of idle rumour) is simply the custodian of the secrets of the hidden possibilities of nature; the master: and guide of her undiscovered potentialities; one who awakens and arouses them into activity by abnormal yet natural powers, and by furnishing them with the requisite group of conditions which lie dormant, and can, rarely, if ever, be brought together if left alone.

25

The Tribune[24]

(Lahore - November 3 and 10)

It would be a mistake, 'like to suppose that the work set on foot by the lamented deceased is confined within the four corners of the Arya Samaj. The principles he preached spread far and wide and created a revolution in men's opinions. Though we do not concur in all that he said and taught, we must agree that he was a man of great abilities genius of a higher order who, by the superior power of his intellect, rose above the gross superstitions inculcated by his own *Śāstras*. * * * We are very glad to observe that his admirers have resolved upon establishing an Anglo-Vedic College in this place perpetuate his memory, It is true that a college of this kind, in order that it might be permanent, would require a respectable fund, but we have every hope the zeal of his numerous admirers will render the

---

[24] The follower of Brahmo Samaj, although Sikh by birth, Sardar Dayal Singh Majidia started the publication of this paper from Lahore on daily basis. After partition, this paper is being published regularly in English and Hindi from Chandigarh. On Nov. 3, it published the news of Swamiji's passing away and on 10th Nov. it published article assessing the life and works of Swami Dayanand.

creation of such a fund perfectly easy. We would suggest that some able disciple of the Swamiji should undertake to write an accurate account of his life- faithful biography of his which, while avoiding all extravagance of thought and style, would present to us all his greatness in their genuine colours.

26
Regenerator of Āryavartta[25]

(Lahore, November 5)

He was what might be called a true reformer. He not only deeply felt for his countrymen and gave vent to his feelings, but, like a true man, he put his shoulder to the task, and bore the burden and heat of the day. Among those to whom posterity will assign a glorious niche in the temple of Fame, Swami Dayanand Saraswati will stand foremost.

---

[25] This paper was an English weekly published from Lahore by Lala Laj Pat Rai, Mahtama Hansraj and Pt. Gurudatta. All the three were its editor.

27

Punjab Times[26]

(Rawalpindi, November 10)

He was a truly and thoroughly patriotic man, which fact alone is, perhaps, enough to entitle him to the lasting gratitude of his countrymen. But he was more. Too vast and profound learning and research, such as very few men have been found to possess since the days of Shankaracharya and his compatriots, he added an amount of energy, intelligence and perseverance, which must be admitted as too rare in mortals of this land in these degenerate days. However we may differ from the principles of his creed and teachings, it would perhaps, be more than churlish not to freely confess that he was one of the greatest men that India has produced, and as such, Indian might well weep for his loss.

---

[26] An English weekly published from Rawalpindi, Pakistan.

28
Indian Spectator[27]

(Bombay, November 18)

With all his faults we looked upon Dayanand as one of the pillars of Āryāvartta. And though we had occasions to differ from him on details of thought and faith, we admired his career none the less on that account. After the death of Sahajananda or Swami Narayan, Gujarat has not produced such a mighty reformer from among the indigenous population as Dayanand. And in natural aptitude and acquirements, as also in the extent of influence exerted, we believe the latter to have by far surpassed Sahajananda Swami. Our contemporaries are not far out in placing him by the aide of the illustrious Shankaracharya. Gifted with uncommon talents, and actuated all his life by singleness of purpose, Dayanand Saraswati has achieved enough good to entitle him to the lasting gratitude of posterity. But the benefit he has conferred on his country has been more or - less of a negative character. He applied his -

---

[27] This was a weekly paper published in English from Bombay. It was edited by Baharam Malabari who was a Parasi reformer.

giant's strength to denouncing idolatry; and terrible were his powers of denunciation as will be conceded by anyone who has witnessed them even once. But the mind, otherwise so well endowed, lacked the constructive faculty. Dayanand's work must, therefore, be considered as half done until someone of his disciples rises after him not only to carry on the crusade against Brahmanic errors but to rebuild the edifice of Vedic truth, the erection of which was the ultimate object of the deceased iconoclast. May Dayanand's mantle descends on any such possible reformer among his pupils is our fervent prayer!

29

Pal Mal Gazette, London
And
Biographical Essays, London,
(1884, pp. 167-171)

(By Friedrich Max Müller)

"He (Dayanand) was a scholar, to begin with, deeply read in the theological literature of his country. Up to a certain point, he was a reformer and was in consequence exposed to much obloquy and persecution during his life, so much so that it is hinted in the papers that his death was due to poison administered by his enemies. He was opposed to many of the abuses that had crept in, as he well knew, during the later periods of the religious growth of India, and of which, as is known now, no trace can be found in the ancient sacred books of the Brāhmaṇas, the Vedas. He was opposed to idol worship; he repudiated caste, and advocated female education and widow marriage, at least under certain conditions. In his public disputations with the most learned Paṇḍits at Benaras and elsewhere, he was generally supposed to have been victorious, though often the aid of the police had to be called in to protect him from the blows of his conquered foes. He took his stand on the Vedas. Whatever was not to be found in the Vedas[28], he declared to be false or useless; whatever was found in the Vedas was to him beyond the reach of controversy. Like all the ancient theologians of India, he looked upon the Vedas as divine revelation. That idea seems to have taken such complete possession of his mind that no argument could ever touch it.

But Dayanand, owing chiefly to his ignorance of English, and in consequence, his lack of acquaintance with other sacred books, and his total ignorance of the results obtained by a comparative study of religions[29], saw no

---

[28] Most of the western scholars are erring on this point. Veda was used as a litmus test for all those bigoted and dogmatic ideas and traditions that crept in the Hinduism in the name of *Sanātana Dharma*. Rishi Dayanand wanted to know the source of these ideas in the Vedas for their authenticity. He never declared the good things and ideas to be false if by chance they are not traceable in the Vedas.

[29] I Think Max Müller did not know that Rishi Dayanand was well aware of other religions and he had done the intensive comparative study of other religions through Hindi translations made available to him by his followers. In Satyarth Prakash, he has dealt with the philosophy of other religions deeply. Only after the comparative study of all religions, he came to the conclusion that Vedas are the real philosophical and

alternative between either complete surrender of all religion or an unwavering belief in every word and letter of the Vedas. To those who know the Vedas, such a position would seem hardly compatible with honesty; but to judge from Dayanand's writings, we cannot say that he was consciously dishonest. The fundamental idea of his religion was a revelation. That revelation had come to him in the Vedas. He knew the Vedas by heart; his whole mind was saturated with them. He published bulky commentaries on two of them, the *Ṛgveda* and *Yajurveda*. He considered the Vedas not only as divinely inspired, or rather expired, but as prehistoric or pre-human. If any historical or geographical names occur in the Vedas, they are all explained away, because, if taken in their natural sense, they would impart to the Vedas an historical or temporal taint. In fact, the very character, which we in Europe most appreciate in the Vedas—namely the historical— would be scouted by the orthodox theologians of India, most of all by Dayanand Sarasvati. In his commentary on the *Ṛgveda*, he had often been very hard on me and my own interpretation of Vedic hymns, though I am told that he never travelled without my edition of the *Ṛgveda*.

---

scientific treatises and not the religious books like that of Bible and Koran.

He could not understand why I should care for the Veda at all if I did not consider it as divinely revealed. While I valued most whatever indicated human sentiment in the Vedic hymns, whatever gave evidence of historical growth, or reflected geographical surroundings, he was bent on hearing in it nothing but the voice of the Brahman. To him not only was everything contained in the Vedas perfect truth, but he went a step further and by the most incredible interpretations succeeded in persuading himself and others that everything worth knowing, even the most recent inventions of modern science, were alluded to in the Vedas. Steam-engines, railways, and steam-boats, all were shown to have been known, at least in their terms, to the poets of the Vedas, for Veda, he argued, means Divine Knowledge, and how could anything have been hiding from that? Such views may seem strange to us, though, after all, it is not so very long ago that a historical and critical interpretation of the Bible would have roused the same opposition in England as my own free and independent interpretation of the *Ṛgveda* has aroused in the breast of Dayanand Sarasvati.

There is a curious autobiographical sketch of his life, published some time ago in an Indian journal. Some doubts, however, have been thrown on the correctness of the English rendering of that paper, and we may hope that Dayanand's pupil, Pandit Shyamaji Krishna Varma, now a BA of Balliol College, will soon give us a perfect account of that remarkable man."

Tributes paid by Bangla Papers

30

Sanjibani[30]

Calcutta, November 3

Attempts were made on his life several times by many evil minded men, but by his own abilities he defied his enemies, and no one could do him any harm. On many occasions, he attracted the admiration of his opponent by delivering excellent speeches. Who is there that can refrain from shedding tears at the death of this admirable man?

[The *Education Gazette*, the *Sulabha Samachar*, the *Gramavrat Prakashika* and other Bengali papers write to the same effect more or less]

---

[30] This was a weekly paper published in Bengali from Calcutta.

Tributes paid by Bilingual Papers

31

Deen Bandhu[31]

Bombay, November 4

Swami Dayanand was a man of great learning and possessed great religious knowledge. His death will prove a shock to all of his relations, friends and disciples, and especially to the religious world.

---

[31] This was a bilingual weekly published both in English and Marathi from Bombay.

32
Subodh Patrika[32]

Bombay, November 4, 1983

Though dogmatic and inconsistent to his religious and social views the Pandit was a man of some originality and did something to revive the interest of our countrymen in the religion of the Vedas. Had he been more self-sacrificing and truth-enquiring than he was, he should have done immense good to the country.

---

[32] Subodh Patrika was a bilingual weekly published both in English and Marathi by Prarthana Samaj of Bombay.

33
Gujarat Mitra[33]

(Anglo-Gujarati Weekly, Surat, November 11)

India has lost one of her foremost of religious reformers of the old school, a rationalistic advocate of Vedic revelation - by the close of a really useful life of our now historical Pandit Dayanand Saraswati Swami, who breathed his last with the dying spasms of the year 1939. Differences may occur as to the preciseness or correctness of his exegetical expositions of the Vedic Scriptures, yet who will not miss on our public platform the deep fervour of his preaching, the great force of his language, the unopposable artillery of his forensic eloquence, the honesty, of the purpose, the firmness of his resolve, his frankness and straightforwardness of his motives; his independence of character and action, and his genuinely patriotic ardent zeal to lift up his country from the depths of superstition and priest-craft, idolatry, and unmeaning ostentatious ritualism.

---

[33]This was a bilingual weekly published in Gujrati and English from Surat, Gujrat.

Tributes paid by Gujrati Papers

34

The Gujarati[34]

Bombay, November 4, 1883

Whatever may be his religious views, his death will damp the spirit of reform that was roused by his establishment of Samajes in different parts of India with their centre in the North. To these associations, his untimely death will give a staggering mow.

---

[34] This was a weekly paper published in Gujrati from Bombay.

35

Jum-e-Jamshed[35]

November 2

Every Native, conversant with the good works of the lamented deceased, will share with us the regret at the untimely death of this great Vedic scholar and well-wisher of India.

---

[35] This was a paper published daily by Parasis in Gujrati from Bombay.

36

The Samachar[36]

Bombay, November 2

The religious views of the Swami were sound and in accord with the Vedic ordinances and the spirit of reform of the present day. He was an inveterate opponent of idolatrous rites and observances, and his main efforts were directed towards their eradication from the Hindu community. He was the principal organiser of Samajes in different parts of the empire, which are established with a view to bringing about a reform in social and religious customs. The death, therefore, of such a learned religious reformer will be a loss to the community. His compatriots should bestir themselves to found some memorial of his illustrious reformer.

---

[36] This was a weekly paper published in Gujrati from Bombay.

37

Vartman Saar[37]

Surat

His untiring efforts for the amelioration of the condition of the Hindu community, his strength of character, and his dauntless moral courage were such as to inspire regard and esteem for him. Crowds went to listen to his masterly languages, which were couched in homely and forcible language. But he lacked the power of arresting the attention of its numerous hearers. His abruptness of manners repelled the advance of his flowers. But whatever may be his faults, there is no denying the fact that the country has suffered by his death, inasmuch as he was mainly instrumental in reviving the dormant religious instincts of the Hindus.

---

[37] This was a weekly paper published in Gujrati from Surat.

38
Vijñāna Vilas[38]

Everybody is acquainted with the name of this great person. We are so sorry to say that this great man has departed to merge with almighty on Oct. 30^{th,} 1883, i.e. on the day of Amavaśyā of Kārttika month, the Tuesday evening.

Dayanand Sarasvati never revealed his original name, the name of his parents, birth place for the fear of being entangled in the mundane world again. That is why proper information regarding this great man is not available. However, he informed that he was born in the state of Morvi in Kathiawar. He was Audichya Brāhamaṇa and belonged to a well to do family. He was born around Vikramī Samvat 1881. This way he left his mortal remains at the age of 58. Swamiji himself informed how he attained education in his childhood, under what circumstances he had to leave his house, how he escaped again on being captured by his father. The story goes like this that after being initiated into Yajñopavit sanskāra at the age of 8 years, Swamiji's father wanted to train him into his

---

[38] This was a news letter of Vidya Guna Prakashak Sabha of Rajkot.

traditional profession. He (Swamiji's father) used to recite *Śiva Purāṇa* himself and also taught the same to his son. Once on the day of Śivarātrī, Swamiji joined the ritual of Śiva Pūjā. He found mice playing over the idol of Śiva and nibbling the offerings made to Śiva. This event was a turning point in his life leading him to disbelieve the idol/*Murti* of Śiva. As ill luck would have it, Swamiji's dearest sister died which made him disbelieve even this mundane world. As per the custom of child marriage prevalent in Gujrat, Swamiji was also subjected to the marriage at his young age. Swamiji opposed this immature marriage and evinced his interest in higher studies in Kashi (Benaras). At this, his father dropped the idea of his marriage. Swamiji found a chance to escaped from his house one night. He passed through Sayala, Kot and Gangad on his way to Siddhpur in search of a spiritual Guru. In the meantime, some monk informed his father about his whereabouts and arrangement to was made to escort him back under the strict vigilance. But Swamiji silently slipped away again. Swamiji studied Vedas on the banks of river Narvada in sChanod Karnali under the guidance of Swami Brahmananda and Swami Purnananda initiated him into Saṁnyāsa and gave him a new name of Swami Dayanand.

For further studies, Swamiji came to Kashi (Benaras) and he studied there Vedas, Nyāya, other Darśanas and the works of Shankaracharya. In those days Brahmo Samaj of Keshava Chandra Sen was very popular in Bengal. Swamiji found that the basic principles of Brahmo Samaj were based on the European concepts. On the way to his visit to Benaras from Gujrat, Swamiji came across many saints, scholars, peripatetic monks and gurus. He found idolatry deeply rooted in Indian society, he also came across a lot of religious bigotry and corruption. Under the prevailing circumstances, Swamiji made up his mind to oust idolatry and bigoted religions (religious sects) from the Indian society. So he first attacked idolatry. The supporters of idolatry came forward to him a fierce opposition. They engaged with Swamiji in disputations. On being defeated in all fronts, they tried to eliminate Swamiji. Under the auspices of Raja Jayakrishna Das, a big conference comprising of 800-900 pundits was convened in Benaras. When Swamiji proved that idolatry was not sanctioned in Vedas, he became very famous and popular in the surrounding area. The social reformers found a great support for them in Swamiji. When the opponents failed to maintain their position in academic debates before Swamiji, they conspire to eliminate him. Once he was poisoned, at other time an attempt was made to slain him with a sword. Swamiji was also once charged with theft, but he got over all these impediments on his way to establish truth. Taking a lecture tour to Hardwar, and Calcutta, he reached Bombay. There also he denounced the practice of idolatry. No one could withstand in front of his arguments. From Bombay, he travelled to Rajkot via Surat, Bharunch and Ahmedabad (presently known as Gandhi Nagar). He made a stop over at Rajkot for 11 days and won over the scholars there to his side with his eloquent speeches. He established an Arya Samaj in Rajkot and proceeded to North India via Ahmedabad and Bombay. By this time, he started his commentary on Vedas and published the same in monthly instalments. He went to Lucknow, Calcutta, Lahore and Mewar. He won over the ruler of Mewar to his side. The ruler of Jodhpur also invited Swamiji when he heard about his name and fame. Swami saved the king from the clutches of a courtesan and counselled him to abolish the corrupt practices prevalent in his court and kingdom. This infuriated many conspirators in the court. They poisoned him. Swamiji fell ill and he had to shift to Ajmer for his treatment. The king put up all his efforts to get the Swamiji treated but all in vain. Though earlier he never consulted any doctor for his ailments, but this time he had to depend upon doctors for his treatment, which also proved fatal for him. Govt. must institute an inquiry into this episode so that the truth may be revealed and the real culprit may be punished. If any inquiry exposes the brain behind this episode, then that person may be held liable for the national loss which not be made up for long. Swamiji had no knowledge of English, but he studied the religious books like Bible and Koran. He used to speak Sanskrit, Hindi and Gujarati fluently. He used to address the common audience in Hindi, so that they may comprehend his actual intention. His delivery was so effective as to leave a permanent impeccable impression on the mind of the audience. He had a towering and majestic personality. Many scholars challenged him in academic debates but they had to withdraw silently. Nobody dared to defeat him in arguments. He was never under pressure and fear while delivering discourses or speeches. He was never conscious of the presence of rulers, officers, opponents and even the Governor General in his audience while delivering addresses. He was among the rarest of rare persons like Shankaracharya.

India has suffered a great loss at his demise. There is no possibility of a birth of person equal to his standing and stature.

Swami Dayanand was endowed with the unique quality of giving solid arguments to prove his point and disapprove his opponent's contention. He confounded his opponents with reasoning and evidence to the extent that they never dared to raise their heads in future. He was able to give a precise answer to the queries imposed before him and this satisfied the inquisitive minds. Dayanand Sarasvati was dead opposed to idolatry, but his opposition was not confined to idolatry, he was also dead against child marriage. He was a staunch supporter of widow remarriage. He deeply investigated the actual condition of his countrymen and the causes underlying them. That is why, he repeatedly emphasised in his lectures upon the social, political and religious reforms. He wanted a healthy and awakened society. He also wanted to abolish the multiplicity of religious sects from India, so that the division among the masses in the country along religious lines may be avoided. He wanted eternal Vedic dharma (values) to replace the different sects and faiths. According to him, child marriage was the root cause of dwarfism, weakness and desideratum of intellectuals in the country. Child marriage was responsible for sexual corruption among widows which led to the evil of infanticide.

Most of these corrupt practices can be prevented by abolishing the child marriage. So he denounced the evil of child marriage rapaciously in his lectures. Casteism is adversely affecting the progress of this country. Due to casteism, people are not able to take part in the progress of country unitedly. Swamiji was very pained by this evil, so he deadly opposed casteism. Indigenously ruled states were infected with many evils. The people had become lethargic, jealous about each other, and drug addicts. Courts were full of courtesans. Kings became ignorant and dominated by the conspirators. Swamiji had a great concern for the indigenous rulers. That is why during his last days he met with the rulers of Udaipur and Jodhpur. Counselled them and reformed them. But as ill luck would have it, this great man could not complete his agenda and fell a prey to the conspirators of these states. He had a burning desire to lead the country to the path of progress, so he never let the issues of polity, education and business go untouched in his lectures. Day and night he was engrossed finding a way out for the progress of the country. We can safely say in the light of his introduction that if he had any desire during his death bed, it was only to see the progress and prosperity of the country.

Where ever Swami Dayanand went and delivered lectures, he established Arya Samajs there. A number of such Arya Samajs as were established by Swami Dayanand is about 100 in the entire country. He delivered more than 300 lectures at different places. He wrote his commentary on *Ṛgveda* till 8th Maṇḍala and on the entire *Yajurveda*. He wrote around 20 books (small and big together) including *Satyārtha Prakaśa*, *Sanskāra Vidhi*, and *Aryābhivinaya*. He referred to 6200 Sanskrit books and 1800 other books composed in Hindi and other vernacular languages in his lifetime. He had no desire to be known as a Guru, although he has more than 300 disciples and thousands of followers. This is no less significant contribution. His desire to bring about unity in the entire country has remained unfulfilled due to his untimely sudden demise. It will be difficult to have a great man like Dayanand Sarasvati. Swami Dayanand was the jewel of the Gurjar land. So we Gujaratis should be proud of him.

Tributes paid by Marathi Papers

39

Sanmarga Dipika[39]

Bombay, November 16

Swami Dayanand had a sincere desire to work for the welfare of his country. He established many Arya Samaj branch and his attempts to prevent the slaughter of kine, together with his many public lectures on the evils of drinking, are too well known. He had a commanding figure, a stentorian voice, and he possessed most of the requisites of an orator.

---

[39] This was a weekly paper published in Marathi from Bombay.

40

The Kesari[40]

Those who cannot tolerate difference in opinion may not, but those who have the admirable patience of appreciating virtue even in their enemy, will admit that Swami Dayanand was gifted with talents and in inquiring turn, and they will say that a great man has departed. Ardent lovers of the Hindu religion ought certain not to have persecuted him so much. Had the times been favourable, the tenets of the Aryan religion would have prevailed over those of Brahmanism. There is no doubt that the Swami could not accomplish much, nor was his erudition properly appreciated; but this was due to our indifference about matters religious. The fact that we have over us rulers of quite a different religion has given perfect liberty to all, and the result is that we ha0ve amongst us thing like a national Church.

[Most other Marathi papers write about the deceased very feelingly].

---

[40] This was a weekly paper published in Marathi from Poona. It was edited by Balgangadhar Tilak. Tilak has remembered Swami Dayanand as a great man while offering tributes.

As to how the news of the Swami's death was received in different parts of Aryavartta and elsewhere, and what his countrymen and foreigners thought of him will be evident from the following;

41

The Rasta Guftar[41]

The efforts put up by Swami Dayanand for the reformation of society were unparalleled in the history. Nobody seems to have such a strong desire for the well-being of society as Swami Dayanand had.

---

[41] This was a paper of Parasi Samaj.

References

1. *Maharishi Dayanand Saraswati kā jīvana carita* by Satyavrata Sharma Dwivedi, Itava, 903
2. *Dayanand Digvijayārka*, Khaṇḍa 3, Farrukhabad, 1887
3. *Arya Magazine*, Lahore Nov. 1983.
4. *Life and Teachings of Swami Dayanand,* 1903.
5. *Rishi Dayanand in the eyes of the West*, published by Indian Foundation for Vedic Science, Delhi, 2006.

Rare Pictures of Swami Dayananda

Seated on Padmasan with cloth wrapped around his chest

Rishi Dayananda made a stop over at Meerut on his way to Hradwar at Kumbh Mela in 1867 (Vikrama Samvat 1924). During his stay at Meerut, this sketch was made. From this sketch, the age of Rishi Dayananda appears to be between 35-40. There is a glow on his face. This sketch was discovered by Yudhisthir Mimamsaka from Meerut while he was searching the Letters of Rishi Dayananda. Its photocopy was published in Arya Gazette, a Urdu paper published from Lahore in Samvat 1983. It was a special issue dedicated to Swami Dayananda.

Seated on the chair wearing a saffron robe and holding a stick with silver handle in his hands

In this picture, Rishi Dayananda has covered his body completely with clothes and holding a stick with a silver handle. This picture was taken in Dehradun either in the month of Kartika or Margashirsh in Nov. 1880 (Saṁvat 1937). From the Biography of Swami Dayananda written by Devendra Babu, it is clear that in Dehradun, Swamiji's photo was taken.

Swami Ji in the pose of Samadhi

This photo was sketched in Meerut in 1879 (Saṁvat 1936). Its copy was printed in the Autobiography of Swami Shraddhananda. It appears that this photo was mentioned by Swami Dayananda in a letter to Shyamji Krishna Verma on January 17, 1879.

**Seated on the ground with turban over head and
holding an open book before him**

In this photo Rishi Dayananda is seen seated on the ground with turban whose tail part is visible outside on the neck. In the front an open book is placed and a stick with a silver knob is lying close by. Swami ji looking weak, as he was suffering from dysentery then. This photo was taken in 1879 (Saṁvat 1936). Its small copy was given to Pt. Bhagvadatta by Mahatama Hansraj. He made a big photo out of it and installed the same in the Lal Chand Library of Dayananda College Lahore.

Seated on a Chair dressed in saffron robes with turban tied over his head

This sketch was made by Babu Harishchandra Cintamani during the time of second visit of Swami Dayananda to Bombay in 1875 (Saṁvat 1932). Mention of this sketch is available at page 4 of *Swami Dayananda Jiwan Charit* by Sh. Devendra Babu. Here it may be pointed out that Harishchandra Chintamani was the manager of Vedabhashya of Swami Dayananda. Since he did some mismanagement with the funds collected for the Vedabhashya, he was fired by Swamiji from this responsibility. Thus he turned rebellion. In this photo Swami Ji has given his side pose.

Front look : Seated on a Chair

This photo was taken in Bombay in 1875 (Saṁvat 1931). In this photo saffron clad Rishi Dayanada is seated on the chair. He has a turban tied over his head also holding a stick. This photo was discovered by Swami Satyananda from Bombay. Since the photo was in dilapidated condition, so feet of Rishi Dayananda are not visible. On the basis of this photo a block was prepared and was printed in the first edition of *'Śrimad Dayananda Prakash'*. This book was available in Lal Chand library of Lahore. From there it was brought at the residence of Pt. Bhagavaddata C Block No. 9, Model Town, Lahore. During the partition it got destroyed along with other literature.

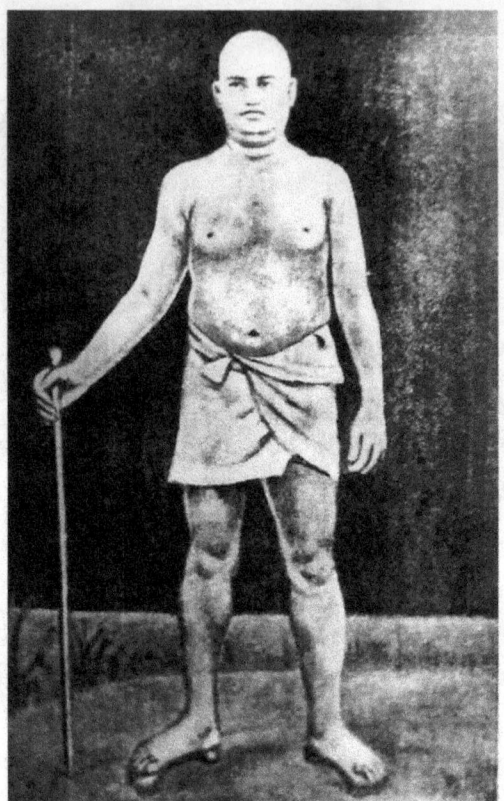

Dayananda as a recluse holding a stick in his hands

This sketch of Rishi Dayananda was taken in Vikrama Samvat 1924 i.e. c 1867 in Hardwar during the *Kumbh Mela* at a place where Pākhaṇḍa Khaṇḍana (extermination of hypocrisy) flag was installed. This is known by the old persons contemporary to Rishi Dayananda. On the basis of this sketch, a big sketch was prepared by an art studio in Poona. This sketch was seen by Yudhisthir Mimansak on 25th December 1926 in the custody of an old gentleman named as Jhunni Lal in Farrukhabad. Similar type of photo was published by Ram Vilas Sarda in '*Arya Dharmendra Jivan*'. The same photo has been published in the '*History of Arya Samaj Lucknow*'. Similar type of photo taken from the original plate was seen by Yudjisthir Mimansak in the custody of Babu Jivan lal S/o Babu Anandi Lal ji master (secretary of Arya Samaj Meerut in 1880). Babu Jivan Lal informed Mimansak ji that this photo was the original photo.

Tributes to Swami Dayanand Saraswati

Seated on the chair with Brahmachari Ramananda

In this picture, Rishi Dayananda is seated on the chair. He is wearing Kharau (wooden shoe). Alongside is standing Brahmchari Ramananda. This photo was taken in Shahpura in the beginning of Samvat 1940. Its dispatch to Ramanand has been mentioned by Swami Dayananda himself in one of his letters addressed to him.

www.ingramcontent.com/pod-product-compliance
Lightning Source LLC
Chambersburg PA
CBHW031450040426
42444CB00007B/1046